23 SONGS TO STRUM & SING

Disney HITS FOR UKULELE

ISBN 978-1-4950-4577-6

The following songs are the property of:
Bourne Co.
Music Publishers
5 West 37th Street
New York, NY 10018

BABY MINE
I'VE GOT NO STRINGS
WHEN I SEE AN ELEPHANT FLY
WITH A SMILE AND A SONG

Walt Disney Music Company
Wonderland Music Company, Inc.
Pixar Talking Pictures

DISTRIBUTED BY

HAL•LEONARD®
CORPORATION
7777 W. BLUEMOUND RD. P.O. BOX 13819 MILWAUKEE, WI 53213

Disney / Pixar Characters and Artwork © Disney Enterprises, Inc. / Pixar

Visit Hal Leonard Online at
www.halleonard.com

Baby Mine

from DUMBO

Words by Ned Washington
Music by Frank Churchill

The Bare Necessities

from THE JUNGLE BOOK
Words and Music by Terry Gilkyson

I could - n't be fond - er _____ of my big home.
and you __ prick a raw paw, _____ next time be - ware.
If you act like that bee acts, _____ you're work - in' too hard.

The bees are buzz - in' in the tree to make some hon - ey just for
Don't pick the prick - ly pear by paw. When you pick a pear, try to use the
Don't spend your time just look - in' a - round for some - thing you want that can't be

me. You look un - der the rocks and plants and take a glance at the
claw. But you don't need to use the claw when you pick a pear of the
found. When you find out you can live with - out it and go a - long not

fan - cy ants, __ then may - be try a few.
big paw - paw. __ Have I giv - en you a clue?
think - in' a - bout __ it, I'll tell you some - thing true:

The bare ne -

ces - si - ties of life will come to you, they'll come to

1., 2.

you! Look for the

3.

you! _____

Bella Notte

from LADY AND THE TRAMP
Music and Lyrics by Peggy Lee and Sonny Burke

Do You Want to Build a Snowman?

from FROZEN

Music and Lyrics by Kristen Anderson-Lopez and Robert Lopez

by.   *(click tongue)*   **ANNA:**
                                                              (knocking)   *(Spoken:)* Elsa?

Verse
Slower, tenderly

3. Please,   I know you're   in   there.   Peo - ple are ask - ing where you've

been.   They say, "Have cour - age,"   and I'm   try - ing   to;   I'm right out

here for you,   just let me   in.   We on - ly have each

oth - er;   it's just   you   and me.___   What are we gon - na   do? ___

___   Do you want to build a   snow - man?

Candle on the Water

from PETE'S DRAGON

Words and Music by Joel Hirschhorn and Al Kasha

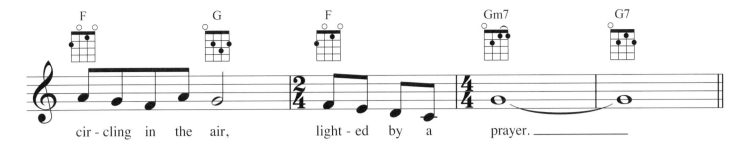

cir - cling in the air, light - ed by a prayer. _____

Verse

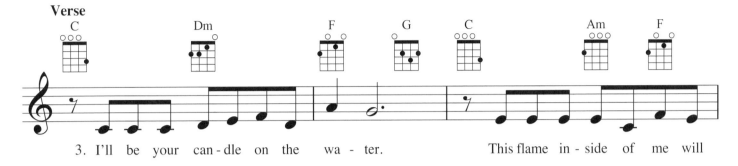

3. I'll be your can - dle on the wa - ter. This flame in - side of me will

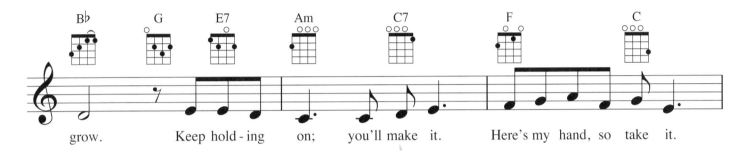

grow. Keep hold - ing on; you'll make it. Here's my hand, so take it.

Outro

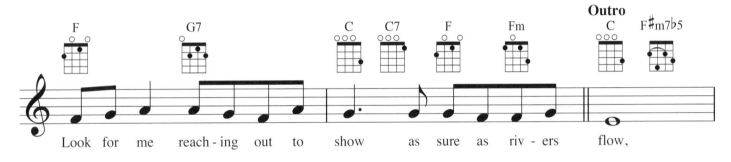

Look for me reach - ing out to show as sure as riv - ers flow,

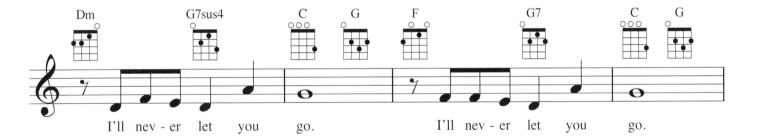

I'll nev - er let you go. I'll nev - er let you go.

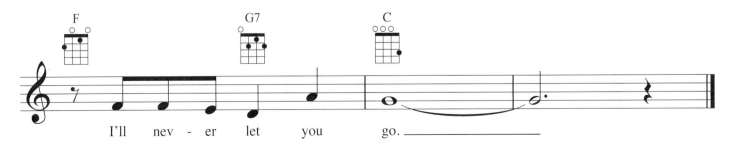

I'll nev - er let you go. _____

Cruella De Vil

from 101 DALMATIANS

Words and Music by Mel Leven

Bridge

first, you think Cru - el - la is the dev - il, _____ but

af - ter time has worn a - way the shock, you come to re - a - lize ___ you've

seen her kind of eyes ___ watch - ing you from un - der - neath a rock. This

Outro-Verse

vam - pire ___ bat, ___ this in - hu - man beast; ___ she ought to be locked ___ up and

nev - er re - leased. ___ The world was such a whole - some place un -

- til _____ Cru - el - la, Cru - el - la De Vil.

Ev'rybody Wants to Be a Cat

from THE ARISTOCATS
Music by Al Rinker
Words by Floyd Huddleston

time he plays! —   But with a square in the act, ___ you can

set mu - sic back ___ to the cave - man days! _   2. I've

Verse

heard some corn - y birds who tried to sing,   but still a
3. Ev - 'ry - bod - y wants to be a cat,   be - cause a

cat's the on - ly cat   who knows how to swing! _   Who
cat's the on - ly cat   who knows where it's at! _____   When

wants to dig a long - haired gig and stuff like that, ___
play - ing jazz you al - ways has a wel - come mat, ___

when ev - 'ry - bod - y wants to be a cat? ___ A
'cause ev - 'ry - bod - y digs a   swing - ing cat! ___

For the First Time in Forever

from FROZEN

Music and Lyrics by Kristen Anderson-Lopez and Robert Lopez

know if I'm e - lat - ed or gas - sy, but I'm some - where in ___ that

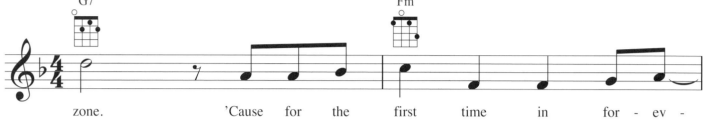

zone. 'Cause for the first time in for - ev -

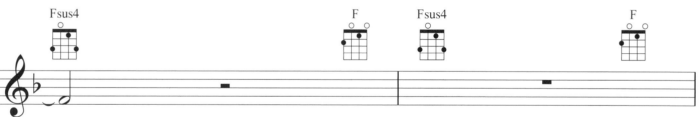

- er, _____ I won't be ___ a - lone. __

Excited again

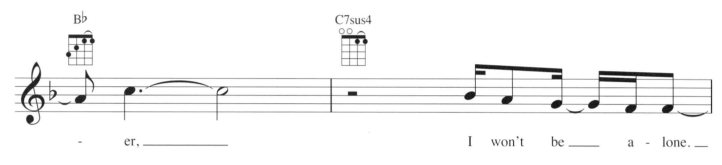

___ *(Spoken:) I can't wait to meet everyone.* *(gasp) What if I meet...*

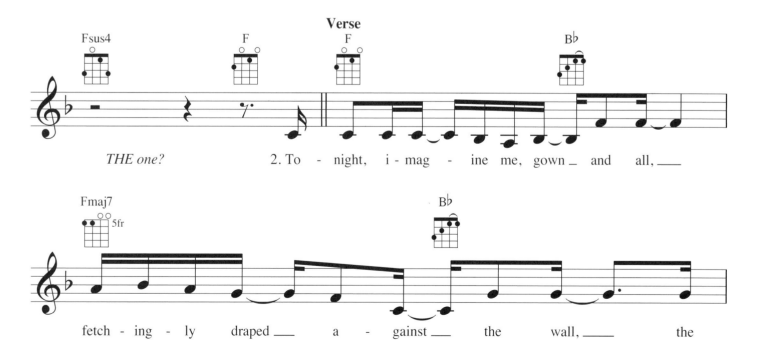

THE one? 2. To - night, i - mag - ine me, gown __ and all, ___

fetch - ing - ly draped ___ a - gainst ___ the wall, ___ the

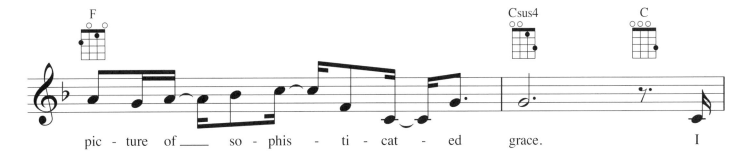

pic - ture of ____ so - phis - ti - cat - ed grace. I

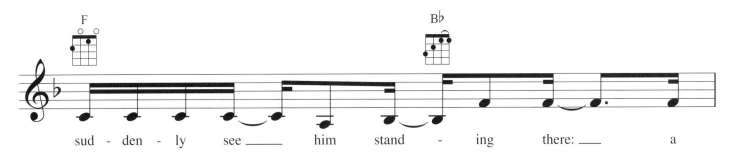

sud - den - ly see ____ him stand - ing there: ____ a

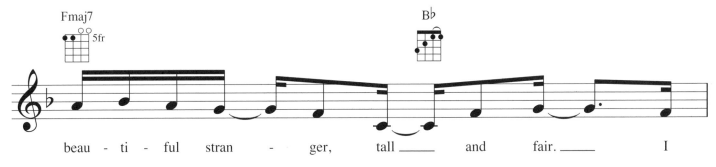

beau - ti - ful stran - ger, tall ____ and fair. ____ I

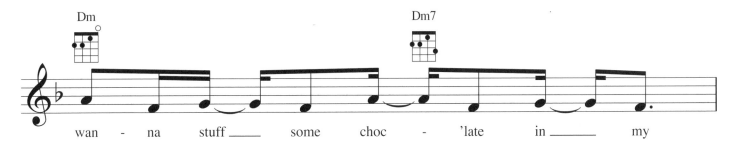

wan - na stuff ____ some choc - 'late in _____ my

face! But then we laugh and talk ___ all eve - ning, which is

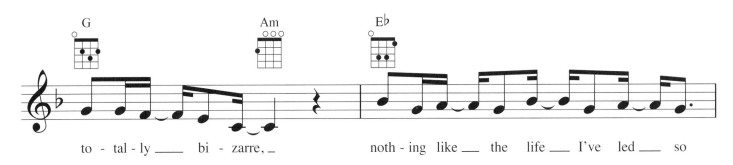

to - tal - ly ___ bi - zarre, __ noth - ing like ___ the life ___ I've led ___ so

Chorus

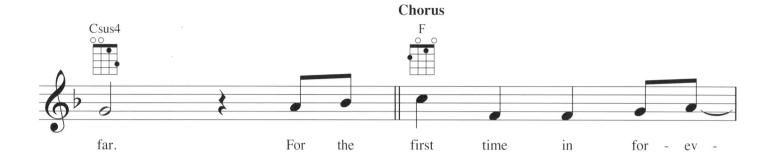

far.   For the   first   time   in   for - ev -

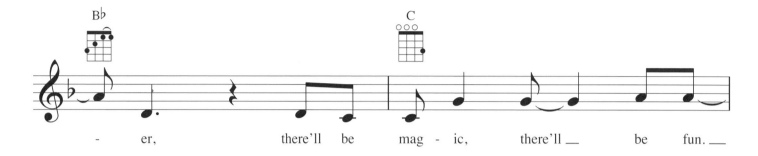

- er,   there'll be   mag - ic,   there'll __ be   fun. __

__   For the   first   time   in   for - ev - er,   I   could be

no - ticed   by __ some - one. __   And   I

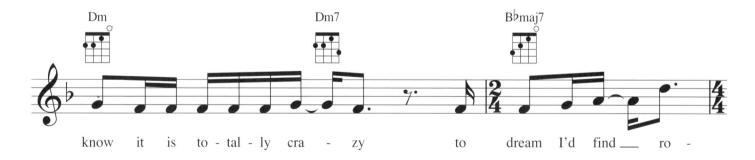

know it is to - tal - ly cra - zy   to   dream I'd find __ ro -

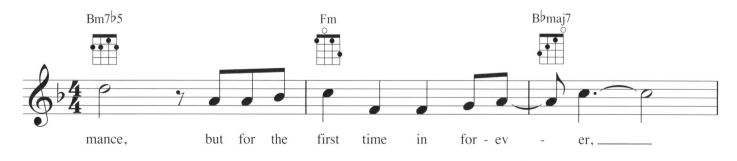

mance,   but for the   first   time in   for - ev - er, __

at least _ I've got _ a chance. _

Bridge

ELSA: Don't let them in; don't let them _ see;

be the good girl _ you al - ways have to be. _ .

Con - ceal, don't feel, put on a show. Make

one wrong move, and ev - 'ry - one will know.

ANNA: It's on - ly for to - day!

But it's on - ly for to - day. It's ag - o - ny to

chance   to   find ___   true   love. ___

con - ceal,   don't   feel,   don't   let   them   I

know   it   all   ends   to - mor - row, _____   so   it

know.

has   to   be ___   to - day.   'Cause   for   the

first   time   in   for - ev - er,   for   the

first   time   in   for - ev - er, _____

noth-ing's   in   my ___   way! _____

He's a Tramp

from LADY AND THE TRAMP
Words and Music by Peggy Lee and Sonny Burke

I See the Light

from TANGLED

Music by Alan Menken
Lyrics by Glenn Slater

Verse
Moderately

Female: 1. All those days, watch-ing from the win-dows. All those years,
2. Now I'm here, blink-ing in the star-light. Now I'm here;

out-side, look-ing in. All that time, nev-er e-ven know-ing
sud-den-ly I see.

1.

All that time, nev-er e-ven know-ing

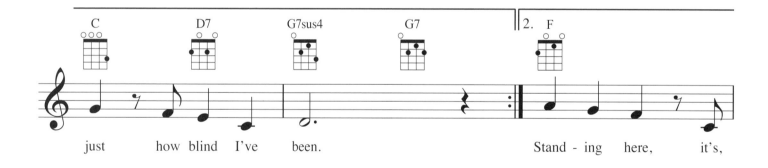

just how blind I've been. Standing here, it's

2. F

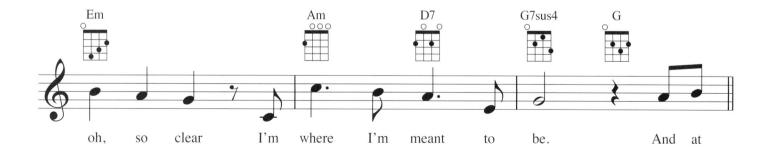

oh, so clear I'm where I'm meant to be. And at

Chorus

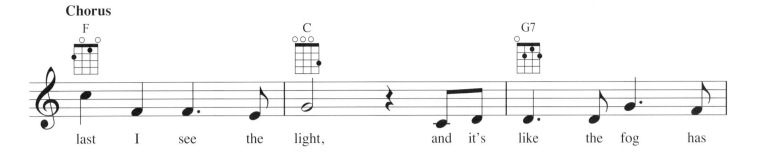

last I see the light, and it's like the fog has

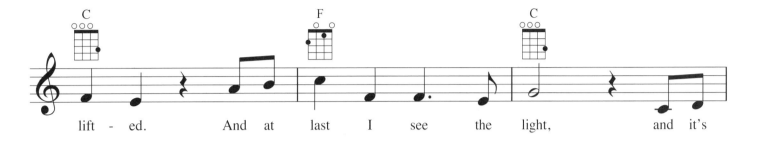

lift - ed. And at last I see the light, and it's

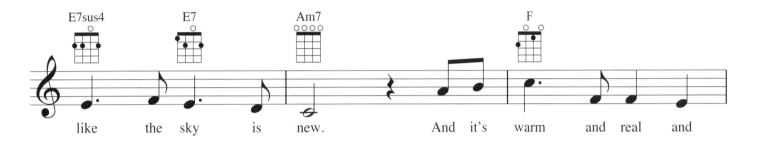

like the sky is new. And it's warm and real and

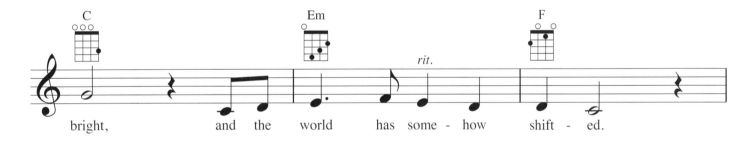

bright, and the world has some - how shift - ed.

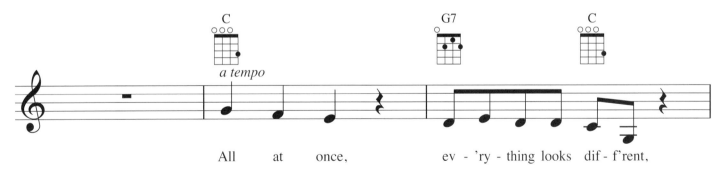

All at once, ev - 'ry - thing looks dif - f'rent,

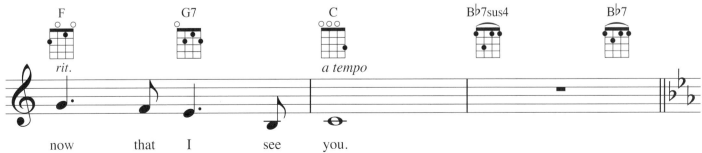

now that I see you.

light, *Female:* and it's like the sky is new. *Both:* And it's

warm and real ___ and bright, ___ and the world has some-how

Outro-Verse
Expressively

a tempo

rit.

shift - ed. All at once,

ev - 'ry - thing is dif - f'rent, now that I see you.

Slowly, freely

rit.

Now that I see

rit.

you.

I've Got No Strings

from PINOCCHIO

Words by Ned Washington
Music by Leigh Harline

Kiss the Girl

from THE LITTLE MERMAID

Music by Alan Menken
Lyrics by Howard Ashman

Chorus

Sha la la la la la, my oh my. ___ Look like the boy too shy. ___ Ain't gon - na

kiss the girl. Sha la la la la la, ain't that sad. ___ Ain't it a

shame, too bad. ___ He gon - na miss the girl. ___ *(Instrumental)*

Verse

3. Now's your mo - ment, float - ing in a blue la - goon. ___

___ Boy, you bet - ter do it soon. ___ No time will be

bet - ter. ___ She don't say a word ___ and she won't ___

Lava

from LAVA
Music and Lyrics by James Ford Murphy

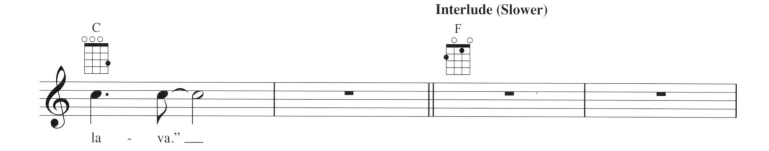

la - va." __

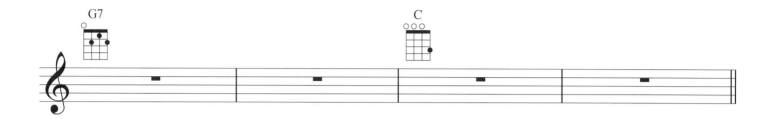

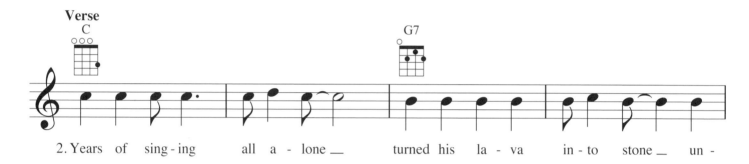

2. Years of sing-ing all a - lone __ turned his la - va in - to stone __ un -

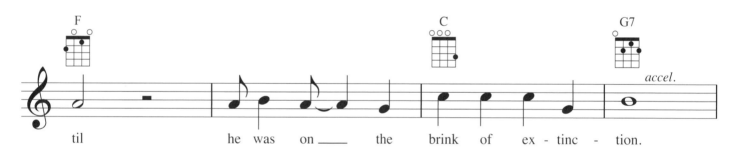

til he was on ___ the brink of ex - tinc - tion.

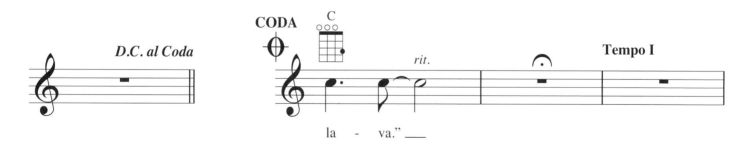

D.C. al Coda

CODA

rit. **Tempo I**

la - va." __

3. Ris - ing from the sea be - low __ stood a love - ly

you.   I ____ wish that ____ the   earth, sea ____ and the   sky   up ____ a -

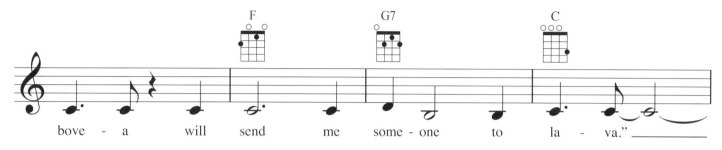

bove - a   will   send   me   some - one   to   la - va." ____

Interlude

a tempo

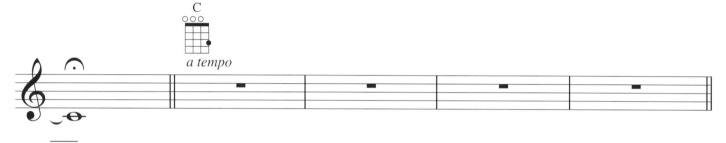

____

Verse

Male: 6. Oh,   they   were   so   hap - py ____   to   fi - n'lly   meet   a -
(7.) long - er   are   they   all   a - lone, ____   with   *a - lo - ha* ____   as

bove   the   sea. ____   All ____   to - geth - er   now ____   their
their   new   home, _   and   when   you   vis - it   them ____

1.

2.

la - va   grew   and   grew.   7. No
this   is   what   they   sing.

Let It Go
from FROZEN
Music and Lyrics by Kristen Anderson-Lopez and Robert Lopez

1. The snow glows white on the moun-tain to-night; __ not a foot-print __ to be seen. __ king-dom of i - so - la - tion, and it looks like I'm the queen. __ The wind __ is howl- -ing like __ this swirl - ing storm __ in - side. __

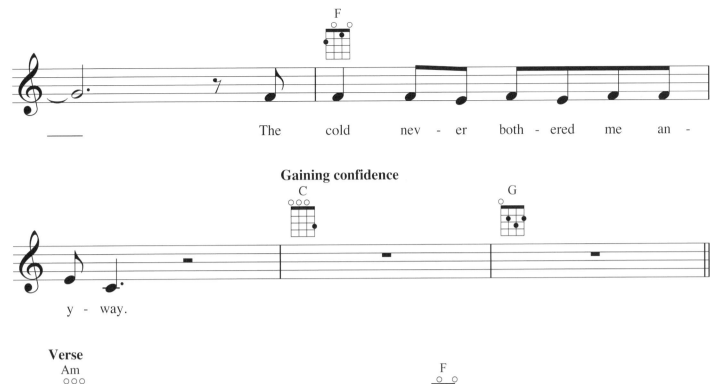

The cold nev - er both - ered me an -

Gaining confidence

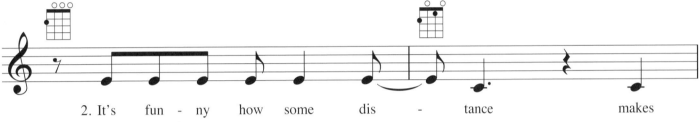

y - way.

Verse

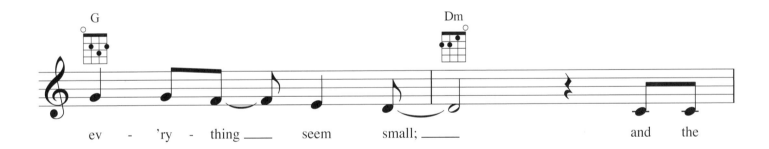

2. It's fun - ny how some dis - tance makes

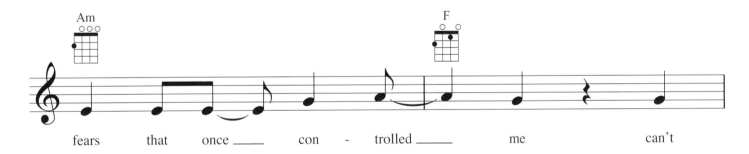

ev - 'ry - thing ___ seem small; ___ and the

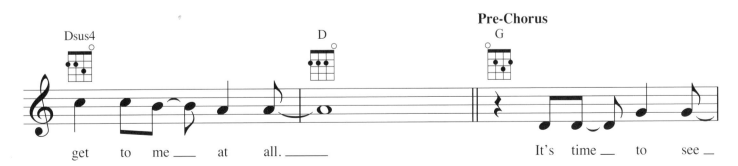

fears that once ___ con - trolled ___ me can't

Pre-Chorus

get to me ___ at all. ___ It's time ___ to see ___

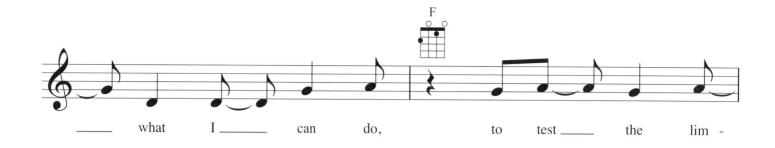

_____ what   I _____ can   do,   to   test _____   the   lim -

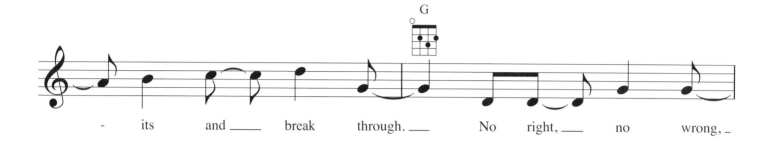

- its   and _____   break   through. _____   No   right, _____   no   wrong, _____

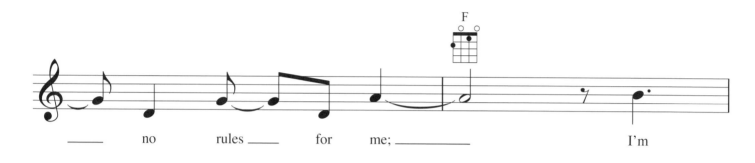

_____   no   rules _____   for   me; _____   I'm

D.S. al Coda

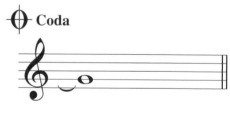

Coda

free! _____   Let   it   go, _____   _____

Bridge

My   pow -   er   flur -   ries   through _   the   air _____

_____   in - to _____   the   ground. _____   My   soul _   is   spi -

-ral - ing _____ in fro - zen frac - tals all _____

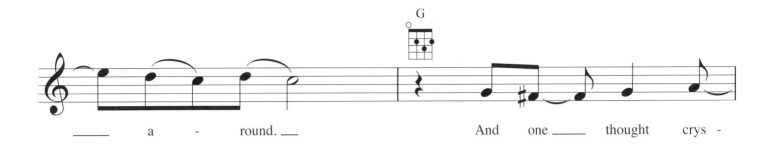

_____ a - round. _____ And one _____ thought crys -

. - tal - liz - es like _____ an i - cy blast: _____

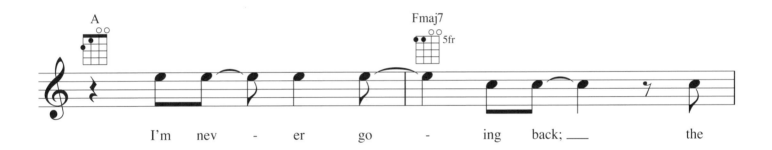

I'm nev - er go - ing back; _____ the

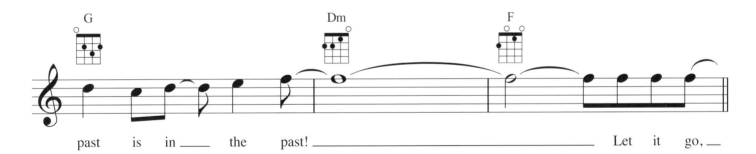

past is in _____ the past! _____ Let it go, _____

Chorus

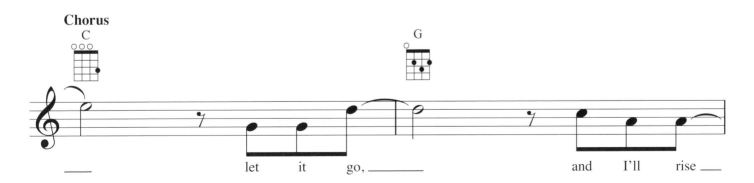

_____ let it go, _____ and I'll rise _____

45

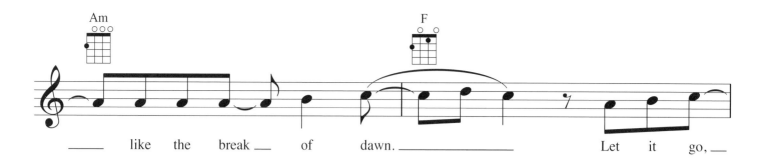

_____ like the break _____ of dawn. _____ Let it go, _____

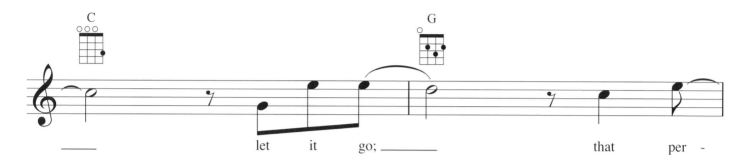

_____ let it go; _____ that per -

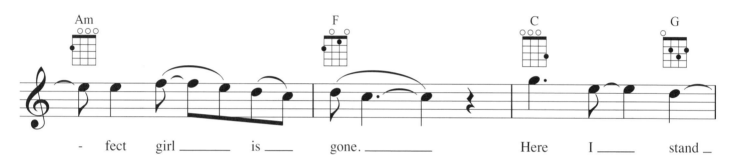

- fect girl _____ is _____ gone. _____ Here I _____ stand _____

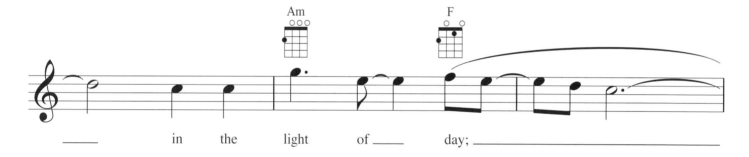

_____ in the light of _____ day; _____

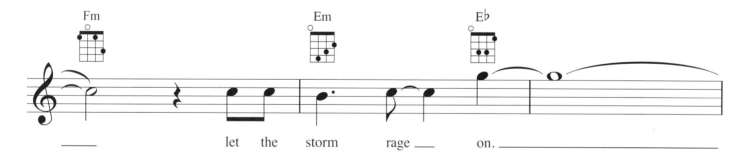

_____ let the storm rage _____ on. _____

_____ The cold nev - er both-ered me an - y - way.

Once Upon a Dream

from SLEEPING BEAUTY

Words and Music by Sammy Fain and Jack Lawrence
Adapted from a Theme by Tchaikovsky

So This Is Love

from CINDERELLA

Lyrics and Music by Mack David, Al Hoffman and Jerry Livingston

True Love's Kiss

from ENCHANTED

Music by Alan Menken
Lyrics by Stephen Schwartz

49

just   find   who   you   love   through   true   love's

Interlude

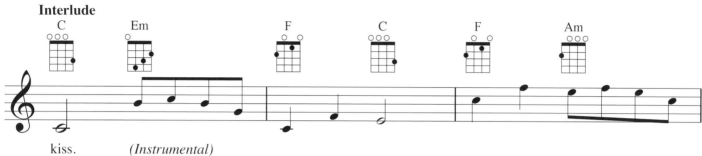

kiss.   *(Instrumental)*

Light Waltz, in one

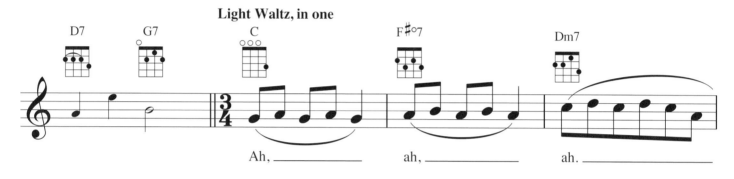

Ah, _____   ah, _____   ah. _____

Verse

__   2. She's   been   dream - ing   of   a   true   love's

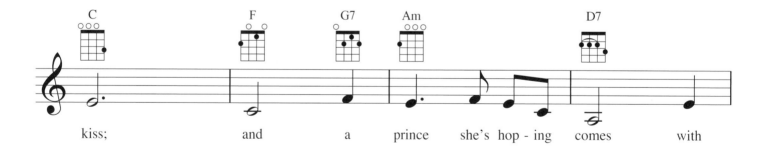

kiss;   and   a   prince   she's   hop - ing   comes   with

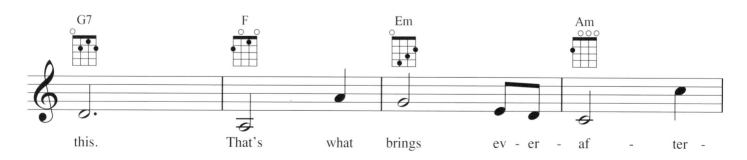

this.   That's   what   brings   ev - er - af - ter -

ings   so   hap   -   py.   *(Instrumental)*

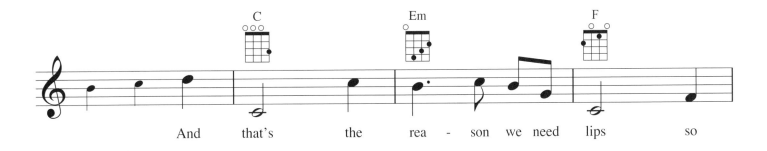

And   that's   the   rea   -   son   we   need   lips   so

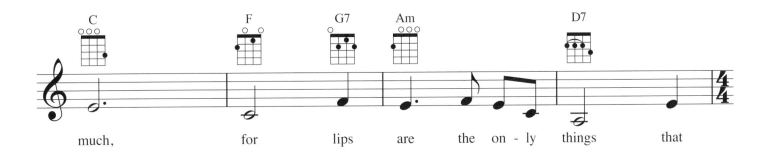

much,   for   lips   are   the   on - ly   things   that

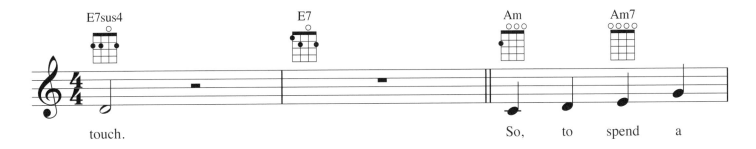

touch.   So,   to   spend   a

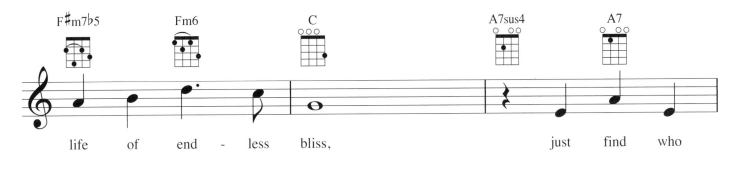

life   of   end - less   bliss,   just   find   who

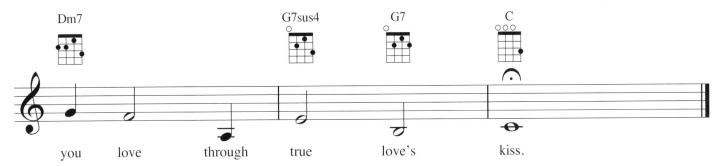

you   love   through   true   love's   kiss.

Under the Sea

from THE LITTLE MERMAID
Music by Alan Menken
Lyrics by Howard Ashman

Such won - der - ful things sur - round you. What more _ is you
One day _ when the boss get hun - gry, guess who _ gon' be

look - in' for? Un - der the sea,
on the plate? Un - der the sea,

Chorus

un - der the sea. Dar - lin', it's
un - der the sea. No - bod - y

bet - ter down _ where it's wet - ter. Take _ it from me.
beat us, fry _ us and eat us in _ fric - as - see.

Up on the shore they work _ all day. _____ Out in the
We what the land folks loves _ to cook. _____ Un - der the

sun they slave _ a - way, while we de - vot - in' full time to
sea we off _ the hook. We got no trou - bles, life is the

Bridge

_____ play the flute. The carp ___ play the harp. The plaice ___ play the bass, and they _

_____ sound - in' sharp. The bass ___ play the brass. The chub ___ play the tub. The fluke _

_____ is the duke of soul. The ray, ___ he can play. The ling's _

_____ on the strings. The trout ___ rock - in' out. The black - fish, she sings. The smelt _

_____ and the sprat, they know ___ where it's at. And, oh, that blow - fish

Interlude

blow.

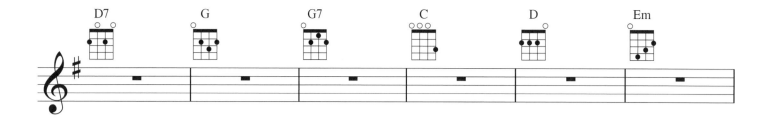

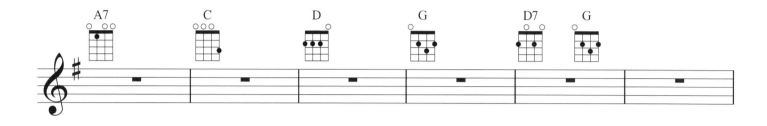

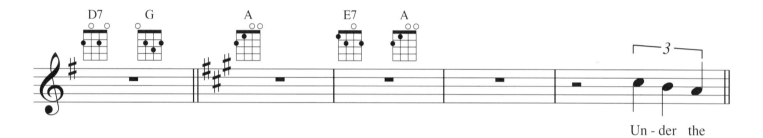

Un - der the

Chorus

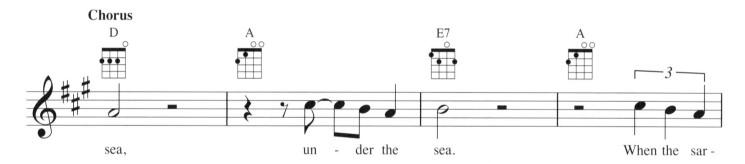

sea,   un - der the sea.   When the sar -

dine be - gin ___ the be - guine, it's mu - sic to me.

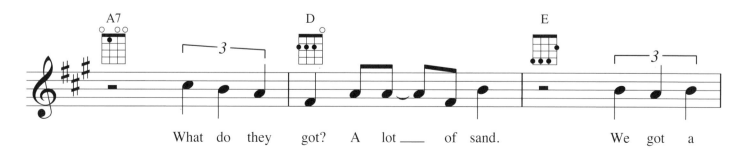

What do they got? A lot ___ of sand.   We got a

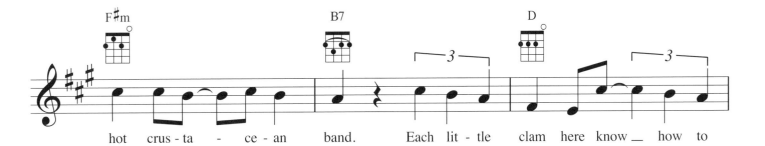

hot crus - ta - ce - an band. Each lit - tle clam here know __ how to

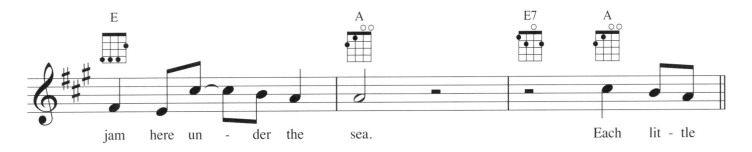

jam here un - der the sea. Each lit - tle

Outro

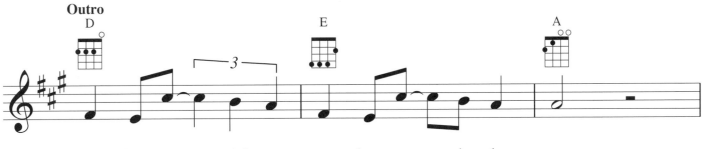

slug here cut - tin' a rug here un - der the sea.

Each lit - tle snail here know __ how to wail here. That's _ why it's

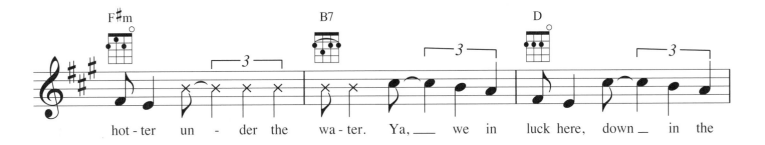

hot - ter un - der the wa - ter. Ya, __ we in luck here, down __ in the

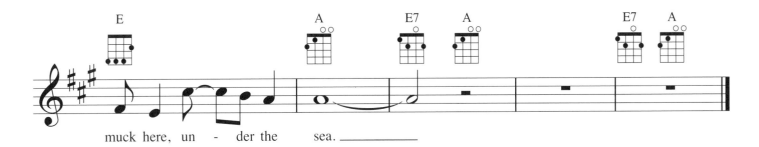

muck here, un - der the sea. _____

When I See an Elephant Fly

from DUMBO
Words by Ned Washington
Music by Oliver Wallace

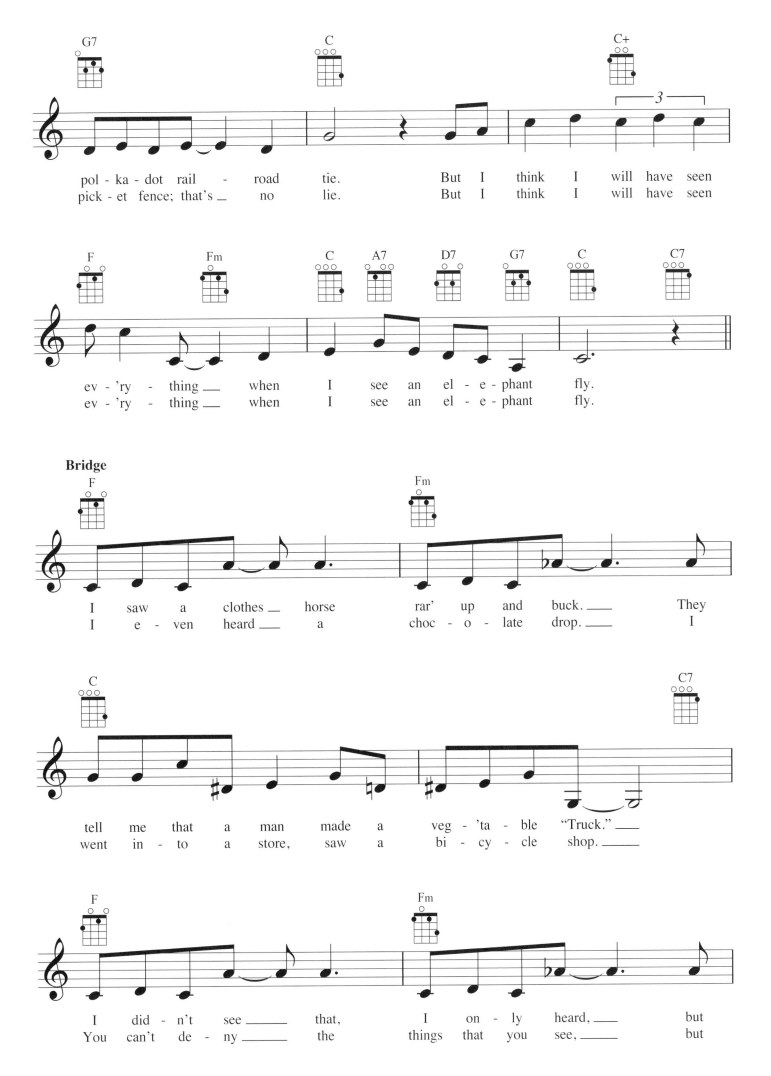

just   to   be   so - cia - ble   I'll   take   their   word. ___ I   saw   a
I   know there's cer - tain things   that   just   can't   be. ____ The oth - er

Outro-Verse

lan - tern   slide, ____   saw   an   old   cow   hide, ___ and   I   just
day   by   chance, __   saw   an   old   barn   dance, __   so   I'm   a

laughed   till   I   thought ___   I'd   die.   But   I
gul - li - ble   sort _____   of   guy.   But   I

3

think   I   will   have   seen   ev - 'ry - thing ___   when
think   I   will   have   seen   ev - 'ry - thing ___   when

1.   **2.**

I   see   an el - e - phant   fly.   2. I   saw   a
I   see   an el - e - phant   fly.

When She Loved Me

from TOY STORY 2
Music and Lyrics by Randy Newman

when she'd say, "I will al - ways love you."

Outro

Lone - ly and for - got - ten, nev - er thought she'd look my way, and she

smiled at me and held me just like she used to do, like she

loved me when she loved me. When some - bod - y loved me,

ev - 'ry - thing was beau - ti - ful. Ev - 'ry hour we spent to - geth - er

lives with - in my heart, when she loved me.

63

A Whole New World

from ALADDIN
Words by Alan Menken
Lyrics by Tim Rice

Chorus

with new ho - ri - zons to __ pur - sue. __ I'll chase them

an - y - where. There's time to spare. Let me share this

whole new world with you. _____ A whole new

Outro

world, _____ that's where we'll be.

A thrill - ing chase, a won - drous place for you and

rit.

me. _____

With a Smile and a Song

from SNOW WHITE AND THE SEVEN DWARFS

Words by Larry Morey
Music by Frank Churchill

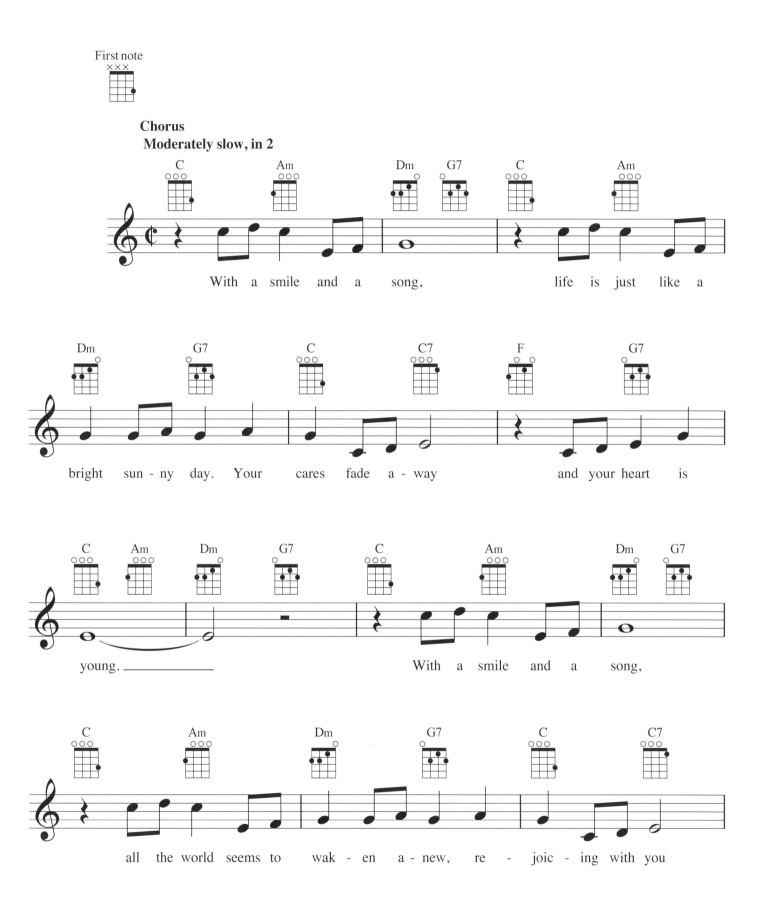

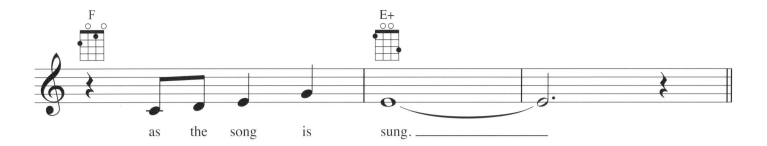

as the song is sung. _____

Bridge

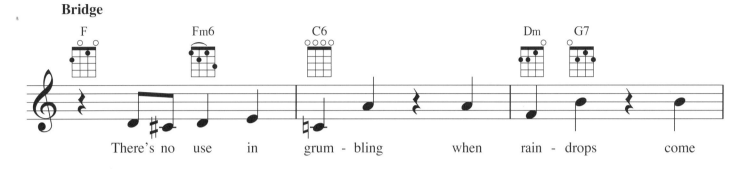

There's no use in grum - bling when rain - drops come

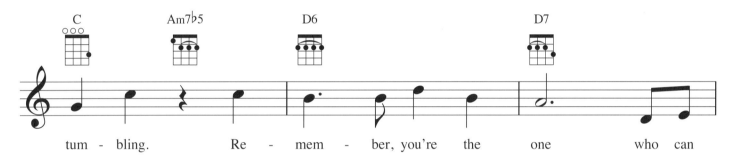

tum - bling. Re - mem - ber, you're the one who can

Outro-Chorus

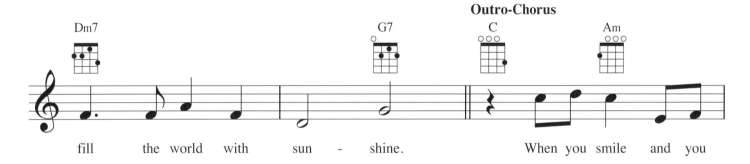

fill the world with sun - shine. When you smile and you

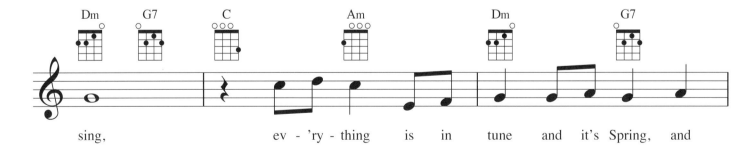

sing, ev - 'ry - thing is in tune and it's Spring, and

life flows a - long with a smile and a song. _____

When Will My Life Begin?

from TANGLED
Music by Alan Menken
Lyrics by Glenn Slater

First note

Verse
Moderately fast Rock

1. Sev-en a. m.,___ the u - su - al morn-ing line - up.
2. Then af -ter lunch, _ it's puz - zles, and darts and bak - ing...

Start on the chores, _ and sweep _ 'til the floor's all clean.
pa - pier mâ - ché, ___ a bit ___ of bal - let and chess...

Pol - ish and wax, ___ do laun - dry, and mop, and shine up.
pot - ter - y and ___ ven - tril - o - quy, can - dle - mak - ing...

Sweep a - then I'll

gain, and ___ by then it's, ___ like, sev - en ___ fif - teen. And so I'll
stretch, may - be sketch, take ___ a climb, sew ___ a dress. And I'll re -

read a ___ book, or may - be two or ___ three; I'll add a
read the ___ books if I have time to ___ spare. I'll paint the

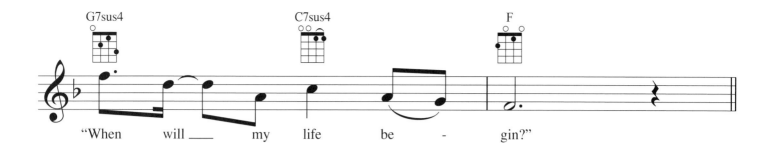

"When will ___ my life be - gin?"

Outro
Slowly, freely

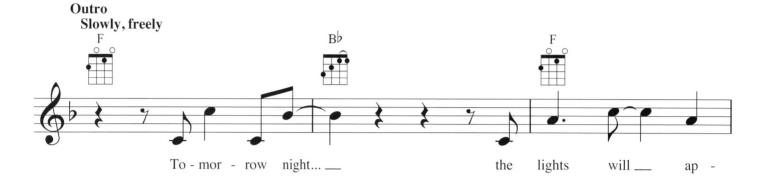

To - mor - row night... ___ the lights will ___ ap -

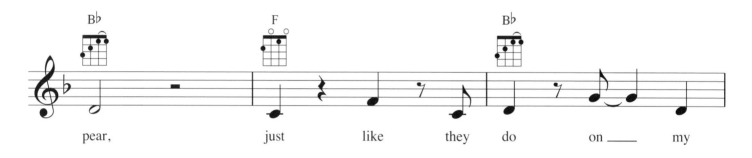

pear, just like they do on ___ my

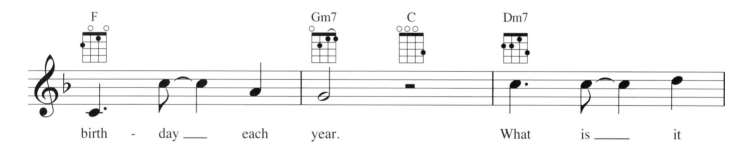

birth - day ___ each year. What is ___ it

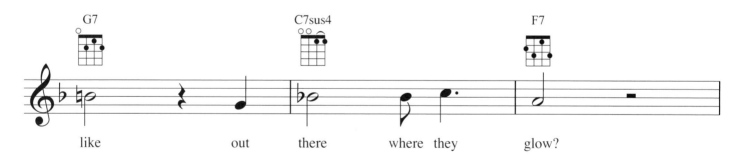

like out there where they glow?

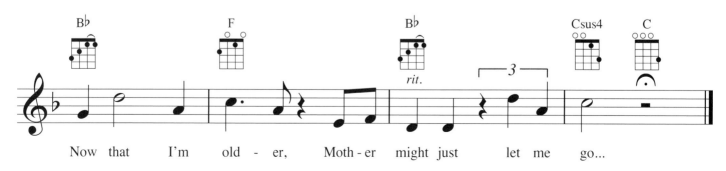

Now that I'm old - er, Moth - er might just let me go...